AF840637

MIND FOOD SECRET

How Nutrition Influences Brain Health, Mood Regulation, Focus, and Mental Performance

SENA LIRASSO

Copyright c 2026 by Sena Lirasso

All rights reserved. No part of this publication may be reproduced, distributed, or transmitted in any form or by any means, including photocopying, recording, or other electronic or mechanical methods, without the prior written permission of the publisher. The only exception is by a reviewer, who may quote short excerpts in a published review. Commercial book summaries are prohibited unless explicitly licensed and/ or authored by the publisher.

Publisher: SenaLirasso@outlook.com

ISBN: 979-8-9961402-2-0 (Paperback)
ISBN: 979-8-9961402-0-6 (eBook)

Cover and interior formatting by KUHN Design Group | kuhndesigngroup.com

CONTENTS

ACKNOWLEDGMENTS

Thank you for choosing to read this book.

In a world filled with noise, opinions, and endless advice, the fact that you took the time to open these pages truly means more than I can express. Reading is an act of intention, and by being here, you have chosen curiosity, care, and hope.

I am deeply grateful for your openness.

I hope that this book helps you see food differently, not as something to fear, control, or perfect, but as a powerful way to support your mind and your overall health. What we eat touches far more than our bodies. It shapes our thoughts, our emotions, our energy, and our ability to feel steady in our lives.

If this book helps you pause before a meal, listen more closely to your body, or choose nourishment with a little more love, then it has done its job.

Change does not have to be dramatic to be meaningful. Small, steady choices made with care can transform how you feel mentally and physically.

Thank you for trusting me with this message.

Thank you for being willing to learn.

And most of all, thank you for giving yourself the chance to feel better, clearer, and more supported.

May this book serve you well now and in the days ahead.

With gratitude,
Sena Lirasso

WHY THIS BOOK EXISTS

This book was written because I have come to realize that what you eat is a big part of how you feel.

The food we eat today is very different from what we ate fifty years ago, and this marked shift plays a large role in our current behavior. All the sugar and chemicals they put in food affect the mind, contributing to anxiety, depression, and mood swings. While these psychological states can be influenced by many different factors, including genetics, stress, trauma, sleep, health conditions, and life experiences, I personally think that food plays a bigger part in the picture than many of us realize.

Here's a clearer breakdown of what a diet looks like when it includes lots of added sugar and ultra-processed foods: Your blood sugar spikes then crashes, resulting in fatigue and brain fog. Such a diet may disrupt your neurotransmitters like dopamine; it can be a major contributor to type 2 diabetes because it causes insulin resistance over time; it also impacts the gut microbiome, which can cause a gut imbalance linked to inflammation, weakened immunity, and even mood disorders.

While I'm not an expert, my passion for this topic began after my 2014 diagnosis of Hashimoto's Disease, which is a chronic autoimmune condition where the immune system mistakenly attacks the thyroid gland. The symptoms can include fatigue, dry skin, constipation, joint pain and stiffness, depression, hair loss, brittle nails, problems with memory or concentration, and muscle weakness. Since then, I've dedicated myself to studying how nutrition impacts the mind as well as exploring the role different foods play in reducing inflammation and improving health. I have read so many books on this topic that I've come to realize that food truly is the best medicine, and if we use it as such, we can overcome a lot of the health issues our society faces today.

I've also observed the effects of food in my personal life, how it can influence the mind in ways no one talks about. Not in extreme cases, but in everyday life. In mood shifts. In anxiety that appears without warning. In foggy thinking. In emotional reactions that feel larger than the moment.

I've also seen it up close in someone I love: my sister, who lives with schizophrenia. Over time, I began to notice something striking. Certain foods and drinks didn't just affect her body. They affected her *entire state*. Her nervousness increased. Her anxiety spiked. Her ability to feel grounded disappeared.

It was astonishing how something as ordinary as food could make a mental illness feel a hundred times heavier.

Yet no one seemed to talk about it. That's why I had to write about it.

THE MISSING CONVERSATION

Most conversations about mental health focus on thoughts, behavior, and medication. Most conversations about food focus on weight, calories, or appearance.

Very few conversations sit in the space between them.

This book lives in that space.

It explores the often-overlooked connection between what we eat and how we think, feel, and function, not in a technical or overwhelming way, but in a human one.

This is not a book about curing mental illness.

It is not a book about blame or control.

And it is not a replacement for professional care. I'm an author who deeply cares about getting the word out to help people get healthier, but I am not a health professional, and you should always consult with your doctor before implementing a new diet.

In the end, this is a book that offers support by increasing our awareness of what we put in our bodies.

THE SECRET MOST PEOPLE NEVER LEARN

Most people believe their thoughts, moods, and daily energy are shaped by stress, personality, or whatever life brings their way. Very few realize something else influences them every single day, food and that it does so quietly, powerfully, and often without their awareness.

I'm not just talking about the simple "eat healthy, feel healthy" way we've all heard before, but in a deeper, more surprising way:

> **Food sends messages to your brain, messages that can sharpen or dull your focus, lift or lower your mood, soothe or stress your nervous system, and strengthen or drain your motivation.**

This is one of the most overlooked truths in modern life. And for me, it isn't just research. It's personal.

For years, I watched my sister live with schizophrenia, and I saw something remarkable, something no doctor ever explained to us:

> **Certain foods and drinks could completely change her day.**

A sugary drink could make her more on edge.

A stabilizing meal could calm her.

Certain processed foods could make her anxiety flare within hours.

A balanced, steady plate could help her feel more grounded and clear-headed.

It wasn't a cure. It wasn't magical.

But it was undeniable.

Even the smallest choices, what she ate for breakfast, how she snacked, whether her blood sugar stayed steady or spiked, affected:

- Her stress levels
- Her nervousness
- Her focus
- Her emotional stability
- Her physical comfort

I saw her body and mind respond to food faster and more dramatically than I ever expected.

And it opened my eyes.

It showed me that food does far more than fuel the body.

> **It shapes the mind's experience.**

Watching her and learning with her made me realize how powerful, delicate, and responsive our inner systems truly are. And somewhere along the way, I began to understand:

> **If food can affect someone with a severe mental illness so deeply, imagine what it's doing to all of us, every day, without us even realizing it.**

That was the moment I knew: The mind-food connection is not a fringe idea.

It's a truth we've simply never been taught.

THE CLUES WE CAN'T IGNORE

In recent years, studies across the world have revealed striking patterns:

- People who consume more ultra-processed foods often report higher levels of depression, anxiety, and low energy.
- Clinical trials show that improving everyday eating habits even in simple ways can lead to better mood and steadier emotional well-being.
- Research on the gut-brain axis has shown that the microbes in your gut create chemical messengers that may influence stress, mood, and focus.
- And balancing blood sugar has been linked to fewer mood swings, cravings, irritability, and moments of fog or overwhelm.

You don't need scientific jargon.

You just need to know this:

> **There is enough evidence and enough real-life experience to confidently declare that food affects how you think, feel, and function.**

Most people have no idea.

But once you see how powerful this connection is, you can't unsee it.

WHY YOU'VE NEVER HEARD IT EXPLAINED THIS WAY

Nutrition is usually taught in extremes:

- Too scientific
- Too medical
- Too restrictive
- Too complicated

But your mind doesn't need complicated rules.

It needs support.

This book is not a textbook, and it's not a diet manual.

It's a guide to the hidden switches inside your body that food turns on and off, everyday switches that shape your calm, your clarity, your emotions, your cravings, and your overall sense of strength and well-being.

These switches are simple.

They are trainable.

And once you understand them, your life begins to feel easier, steadier, and more in your control.

THIS BOOK IS NOT ABOUT DIETING

You won't find guilt or perfection here.

You won't find strict plans or long lists of "do's" and "don'ts."

Instead, you'll learn:

- Why certain foods make you feel clear-minded while others make you feel scattered
- How to steady your mind with simple daily choices
- How to break the cycle of afternoon crashes, cravings, and stress eating
- How your gut talks to your brain
- How sleep, mood, and blood sugar connect
- How to build habits that last because they *feel good*

My goals are simple:

To help you understand yourself better; to help you feel better; and to guide you back to the version of yourself that feels clear, balanced, and whole.

A NEW WAY TO SEE YOUR LIFE

As you move through these chapters, you'll start to notice patterns you've never seen before:

- Why some days feel smooth and others feel heavy.
- Why certain meals calm you.
- Why others jitter your nerves.
- Why stress feels louder after certain foods.
- Why you have cravings even when your stomach isn't hungry.
- Why you sometimes feel "off" without knowing why.

These aren't mysteries.

They're messages.

By the end of this book, the "Mind-Food Secret" will be obvious and deeply empowering.

You'll have simple tools to support your brain, your body, and your emotional well-being every day.

And perhaps most importantly…

You'll never again underestimate the quiet power of what you put on your plate.

CHAPTER 1

THE MIND-FOOD SECRET

"Your body adapts to what you eat. Your mind adapts to what you consume. Your soul adapts to what you love. What you feed yourself today is who you become tomorrow."

JAMES CLEAR

Many believe that their mental state is dependent only on their habits, stresses, personality, or life situations. And while those things shape us, there's a missing piece almost no one explains clearly:

Your brain runs on the raw materials you feed it.

Not metaphorically.

Not spiritually.

Literally.

Every thought you think, every mood you feel, every decision you make, and every ounce of motivation you do or do not have is influenced by what your body does with the food you give it.

This is the "Mind-Food Secret"

Your mind is not floating above your body. Your mind is *fed* by your body.

When you understand this, things that never made sense before suddenly click into place.

WHY THIS SECRET STAYS HIDDEN

The reason people don't know this truth is simple:

> **No one has ever broken it down in a way that feels *useful.***

We hear:

- "Eat healthy."
- "Avoid junk food."
- "Don't eat too much sugar."

But no one tells us why certain foods make us feel clear while others make us feel foggy... or why one meal gives us steady focus and another sends us spinning into cravings... or why stress hits harder when we're tired and under-fueled.

We were taught to think of food in terms of calories, weight, or willpower.

We were never shown how food is integral to mental health, directly impacting our brain structure, function, and chemistry. So, of course, most people feel confused. They blame themselves when their energy crashes or their mood dips. They also assume they're the problem.

But here's what I want you to know, right here in Chapter 1:

> **It's not you. It's your input.**

And when you change the input, your experience of life can change dramatically.

A SIMPLE TRUTH THAT CHANGES EVERYTHING

Your brain has only one job: **to keep you alive and functioning.**

But it can only do that with the materials it's given.

If the brain receives steady fuel, enough nutrients, balanced energy, and supportive signals from the gut, your mind tends to feel:

- Clear
- Calm
- Motivated
- Stable
- Connected
- Strong

When the brain receives unstable fuel, rapid spikes and drops in blood sugar, inflammatory signals, or stress messengers, the mind often experiences:

- Fog
- Irritability
- Anxiety
- Low mood
- Cravings
- Distraction
- Exhaustion

People blame themselves for these experiences.

But many of these shifts are not character flaws, they're biological responses.

Think of it this way: If your phone keeps shutting down at 30%, you don't ask, "What's wrong with my personality?" You ask, "What's going on with the battery?"

Your brain has a battery, too.

This book shows you how to keep it charged.

WHAT THIS BOOK WILL HELP YOU SEE

By the end of this chapter, and especially by the end of this book, you will understand:

- Why your mind feels different on different days
- Why certain foods make you feel calm and others make you feel wired

- Why your focus rises or falls after meals
- Why some eating patterns leave you confident and grounded
- Why cravings appear even when you're not hungry
- Why stress is easier to manage when you eat a certain way
- Why your mornings, afternoons, and evenings each have their own "food rhythm"
- Why emotional eating is not about weakness
- Why willpower is never the full story

You will begin seeing your mind through a new lens, not as something "mystical" or unpredictable, but as something incredibly responsive and trainable through the way you nourish your body.

YOU DON'T NEED PERFECTION

This book is about small shifts, not strict rules. Just a few gentle changes in how you feed your brain can lead to:

- A clearer morning mind
- Fewer afternoon crashes
- Better sleep
- More stable emotions
- Fewer cravings
- More consistent motivation
- A calmer, more centered outlook
- A body that feels supported rather than stressed

When your brain gets what it needs, the rest of your life becomes easier. Not perfect, just easier.

And easier is what creates momentum.

Momentum is what creates change.

And change is what creates a new version of you:

You, but steadier. You, but clearer. You, but stronger.

TOP BRAIN-BOOSTING IDEA

Fatty Fish (Wild Salmon, Sardines, Mackerel) Rich in Omega-3s, crucial for brain cell structure and communication, improving memory and focus.

Idea: Wild Salmon. Put lemon, Redmond's salt, olive oil, and garlic powder on top of the salmon, and bake for 15 minutes at 350 degrees. You can also prepare a salad from it. Immediately after the salmon is cooked, place it on your preferred greens, add more lemon and olive oil, and your preferred vegetables. Sardines or mackerel are other elements to add to a salad with your favorite vegetables. An excellent choice for dinner or lunch.

CHAPTER 2

YOUR BRAIN IS HUNGRY

"The food that enters the mind must be watched as closely as the food that enters the body."

PAT BUCHANAN

If you've ever wondered why you can feel "off" after a meal, foggy in the afternoon, or unusually emotional when you skip breakfast, there's a reason, one most people have never been told:

Your brain is the hungriest organ in your entire body.

Even though it weighs only about three pounds, the brain uses more energy than your muscles, your heart, and every other organ combined.

Every thought, every emotion, every decision, it all happens in your brain, which in turn is powered by the food you eat.

This simple truth explains so much about why your mind can feel dramatically different from one day to the next.

YOUR BRAIN NEVER TAKES A BREAK

Your muscles can rest.

Your voice can rest.

Your digestive system gets breaks between meals.

Your brain?

It's working around the clock.

Even while you sleep, it's:

- Sorting memories
- Repairing cells
- Resetting hormones
- Strengthening connections
- Clearing out waste
- Preparing you for the next day

Your brain uses up to 20–25% of the body's energy just to keep you alive and functioning.

That means:

- When your brain gets steady fuel, you experience clarity and calm.
- When the fuel is unstable, you experience fog, irritability, anxiety, or low motivation.

You're not moody or unfocused because you're "just like that."

Your brain might simply be under-powered.

THE BRAIN HAS A FUEL PREFERENCE, AND IT'S SIMPLE

Your brain's favorite fuel is steady, stable glucose, the kind that comes from whole foods, balanced meals, and consistent energy.

This is why:

- A sugary drink can make you feel wired, then tired
- A pastry can boost mood briefly, then cause a crash
- A protein-rich breakfast can stabilize your energy
- A meal with fiber, color, and healthy fats can keep you calm

Your brain does not like extremes.

Your brain likes a gentle, even supply of energy, not spikes and crashes.

When your energy spikes too high (like after a sugary or ultra-processed snack), you feel momentary excitement, but then your brain gets overwhelmed, and your body quickly pushes the spike down. The result? You end up feeling foggy, anxious, hungry and drained.

When your energy dips too low (like when you skip meals or eat something that doesn't sustain you), Your brain panics, and stress hormones rise. You also feel irritable, emotional, or low, and your cravings appear, and your focus disappears.

Most people think this is "just life."

It's not.

It's fuel instability.

WHY YOUR MIND FEELS DIFFERENT AT DIFFERENT TIMES OF DAY

Have you noticed that your brain has patterns?

- Mornings: clearer or foggier
- Late mornings: productive or distracted
- Afternoons: focused or exhausted
- Evenings: calm or overwhelmed

These shifts often have less to do with your personality and more to do with what and when you last ate.

Here's a simple breakdown:

Morning

If you start your day with a stabilizing meal, your brain stays anchored. To help you feel more stable in the morning, try eating a protein-rich breakfast that can include egg, yogurt, or even a protein smoothie. Add some healthy fats and fiber, like avocados, nuts, or berries. Also drinks lots of water.

Avoid sugary breakfast items like cereals, breakfast bars, and pastries.

I usually find myself eating an avocado and a few berries for breakfast. It's quick and easy.

If you skip meals or eat something that spikes your blood sugar, your day becomes harder.

Afternoon

If lunch is imbalanced or too sugary, you feel that 2 p.m. crash every time. Have a balanced snack like a handful of nuts or boiled eggs instead.

After a heavy carb lunch (or no lunch at all), your energy will crash. Eat a balanced lunch, something that might include chicken, fish, or even some red meat. Have some vegetables and half of a sweet potato. I usually eat more for lunch than breakfast and dinner.

Low fuel means low patience, low motivation, and high cravings.

You're not lazy. You're low-powered.

Evening

At the end of the day, your brain is tired, and if your energy has been unstable, it shows up as overwhelm and lots of cravings.

If you arrive at dinner depleted, you're more likely to stress eat or overeat. Instead, make your intention to eat lighter at dinner, maybe a protein with some vegetables. Avoid sugary or processed foods, as they will affect your mood and sleep. After dinner, I enjoy taking a walk or working out at the gym, since exercise is a powerful way to support mental clarity and overall well-being. The gym is not all about big muscles and weights. Nowadays, they offer classes like yoga, cycling, and even dance. So get out there and get healthy.

If your energy is stable, evenings will feel peaceful instead of chaotic, as will the rest of your days. Imagine how different you will feel with a better understanding of your brain's fuel rhythm!

YOUR BRAIN SENDS "FOOD MESSAGES" YOU JUST HAVEN'T BEEN TAUGHT TO RECOGNIZE THEM

Your mind speaks through sensations, not sentences.

It says:

- "I need steadier fuel" through irritability
- "I'm overwhelmed" through anxiety
- "I'm underpowered" through fatigue
- "I'm stressed" through cravings
- "I'm inflamed" through brain fog
- "I'm running low" through shakiness or mood dips

You've felt these messages your entire life.

You just didn't know what they meant.

Once you learn the language, you will realize:

Your body has been communicating with you for years.

YOUR BRAIN IS NOT AGAINST YOU, IT'S PROTECTING YOU

When you feel scattered or emotional, your brain isn't failing.

It's trying to protect you with the fuel it has.

Think of your brain like a smart, loyal assistant: It wants you to succeed. It makes you feel steady. It wants you to function well.

But it can't perform at its best if it's running on fumes. It can't remain grounded and steady if it's dealing with spikes and crashes. It can't remain calm if it's fueled by foods that create stress signals.

The moment you begin supporting it, even in small ways, your mind responds quickly. Sometimes shockingly quickly.

Many people feel a difference in just a few days:

- More clarity
- More calm
- Fewer cravings
- Better sleep
- More stable emotions

This isn't magical.

It's biology finally working *with* you instead of against you.

WHY THIS MATTERS FOR YOU

Everything you want, peace, clarity, focus, better habits, a more stable mood, depends on your brain having consistent support.

You deserve a mind that feels steady.

You deserve energy that lasts.

You deserve days that feel manageable instead of overwhelming.

And you deserve to understand what's been happening inside you all along.

TOP BRAIN-BOOSTING IDEA

Leafy Greens (Spinach, Kale, and Broccoli) are packed with folate, vitamin K, lutein, and beta-carotene, which help slow cognitive decline.

Idea: Sauté greens in a pan with olive oil, Redmond's salt, garlic, and lemon. Or make a salad with either one. Add in a protein, and it's great for a healthy lunch or dinner.

CHAPTER 3

THE SIX HIDDEN SWITCHES THAT CONTROL YOUR DAY

"Everyone is in such a good mood when they've eaten well."

E.A. BUCCHIANERI

A few years ago, I started recognizing something that changed how I saw food forever. It wasn't a study or a headline. It was a pattern, friends, family, even strangers would describe their days using the same phrases:

- "I don't know why I snapped."
- "I just couldn't focus."
- "I felt anxious for no reason."
- "I was fine . . . and then suddenly I wasn't."
- "I had zero energy, and I don't know why."

At first, it sounded like stress. Or life. Or personality. But when I started to investigate the circumstances behind these "mysterious" emotional states of mind, asking people about what they'd eaten (or hadn't eaten) before they ending up feeling like this, the truth began to become clear.

The shift almost always followed food.

That's when I realized something important: food doesn't just fuel the body, it also flips switches. It has the power to influence how we think, feel, and function, quietly shaping our energy, focus, and mood in ways we often overlook.

A DAY THAT FEELS FAMILIAR

Picture a typical day. You wake up already feeling tired, but you push through, assuming it's just part of life because you're getting older. Your breakfast is rushed or even skipped, so your body starts the day without any fuel. By mid-morning, your thoughts begin to feel scattered, making it harder to focus or stay on track. Lunch gives you a brief lift in energy, but it doesn't last, especially if you've only consumed something processed or sugary, and soon after, you experience a heavy crash that leaves you feeling sluggish and mentally foggy. As the afternoon sets in, irritability creeps in, and you feel like everything bothers you, even things that normally wouldn't. Then your hunger increases, cravings start to kick in, and you're craving something sweet, like the biggest piece of cake you can find. By evening, your patience wears thin, your energy is depleted, and even simple decisions feel overwhelming.

Most people blame this kind of day on all the demands it's made of you. But the truth is, your body has been responding to the fuel it's been given all along, quietly flipping internal switches that influence your energy, mood, focus, and cravings. The challenge is that most of us were never taught that those switches exist, let alone how to support them.

MEET THE SWITCHES

Inside your body are six powerful systems that respond to what you eat.

When these systems are supported, your mind feels clear and steady.

When they're stressed, your mind gets rattled, which means that even if your life looks "fine," it doesn't feel fine to you.

These are the six hidden switches:

1. Blood Sugar
2. Inflammation
3. Gut Signals
4. Brain Chemicals
5. Stress Hormones
6. Energy Production

You don't need to master them.

You just need to recognize them.

Once you do, so many confusing moments in your life will suddenly make sense.

Switch #1: Blood Sugar: The Mood Rollercoaster

I once heard someone say, "I'm either totally fine… or completely overwhelmed."

That's blood sugar talking. When blood sugar spikes too fast and drops too hard, the brain panics. Stress hormones rise. Mood swings appear. The focus disappears.

People call this:

- Being "hangry"
- Being emotional
- Having no patience
- Feeling shaky or anxious

But it's not a character flaw. It's an unstable energy signal.

When blood sugar stays steady, your mood often does too. Stabilizing your blood sugar start with building meals that provide steady, lasting energy. Focus on combining protein, (chicken) healthy fats (avocado), and fiber (vegetable or berries). Meals like these slow down how quickly sugar enters your blood stream and keep you feeling full and clearheaded. Instead of processed ones, choose whole foods like eggs, meat, chicken, vegetables, fruits, nut, seeds, and balanced carbohydrates such as sweet potatoes or whole grains. Eating regularly without skipping meals also prevents dips. It is perhaps most important to limit your intake of things that are highly sugary and ultra-processed (I call it fake food) since they can trigger sharp rises in your blood sugar, followed by a sudden crash.

When you consistently fuel your body this way, you'll see a big difference in your focus, energy, and emotional stability.

Switch #2: Inflammation: The Fog Amplifier

Some foods quietly irritate the body. Not enough to make you sick, but enough to make you feel heavy, foggy, or off.

People describe it as:

- "My head feels thick."
- "I can't think clearly."
- "Everything feels harder."

Diet-induced inflammation is a persistent, low-grade immune response triggered by specific nutrients and chemicals in certain foods. Unlike the swelling you see from a cut, this metabolic inflammation occurs internally, often affecting your gut health and blood vessels before symptoms even appear.

When inflammation rises, the brain works harder just to think. Inflammation in the body is heavily influenced by the food we eat. Ultra-processed foods such as refined sugars, sugary drinks, white flours, fried foods, and processed meats, can promote ongoing inflammation by disrupting blood sugar balance and placings lots of stress on the body. Not only do these foods lack the nutrients your body needs to repair itself, they also damage it, unbalancing your hormones, your mood, and your health. So why eat these fake foods? It is time to switch to whole foods to help calm and regulate inflammation. Foods rich in antioxidants and healthy fats, like greens, berries, fatty fish, nuts, seeds, and olive oil, support the body's natural ability to heal and protect you.

When inflammation lowers, clarity returns.

Most people never connect the two ideas: that some foods inflame the body while other foods lower inflammation.

Switch #3: Gut Signals: The Second Brain Conversation

Your gut isn't silent.

It sends messages to your brain all day long.

Signals about safety, stress, and balance.

When your gut is supported:

- Your nervous system feels calmer
- Your mood feels steadier
- Your body feels grounded

When your gut is irritated:

- Anxiety feels louder
- Stress feels heavier
- Sleep suffers

People say, "I feel it in my gut" for a reason.

Switch #4: Brain Chemicals: The Motivation Makers

Your brain uses chemicals to help you feel motivated, calm, connected, and focused.

Those chemicals don't appear out of nowhere.

They're built from nutrients.

When the building blocks are missing:

- Motivation drops
- Joy feels muted
- Focus becomes difficult

This isn't about happiness, it's about support.

Switch #5: Stress Hormones: The Survival Alarm

When fuel is low or unstable, your body flips into survival mode.

Cortisol rises.

Adrenaline spikes.

Your body thinks something is wrong.

You feel:

- On edge
- Wired but tired
- Unable to relax

Food can either calm this alarm … or keep it ringing all day.

Switch #6: Energy Production: The Brain's Battery

Your brain cells need tiny power stations to create energy.

When those power stations struggle:

- Mental fatigue appears
- Motivation disappears
- Focus fades quickly

You can sleep eight hours and still feel exhausted if this switch isn't supported.

WHY THIS CHANGES EVERYTHING

Once you know these switches exist, you stop asking:

"What's wrong with me?"

And you start asking:

"Which switch needs support right now?"

That question changes everything.

Instead of self-blame, you gain awareness.

Instead of frustration, you gain clarity.

Instead of chaos, you gain calm.

A NEW WAY FORWARD

You don't need to fix all six switches at once.

You don't need perfection.

You only need to support them gently, consistently, and with understanding.

TOP BRAIN-BOOSTING IDEA

Nuts (Walnuts) offer vitamin E, healthy fats, and plant-based omega-3s that help fight oxidative stress.

Idea: A handful of walnuts with a tablespoon of coconut oil, topped with some blueberries. A great healthy dessert!

CHAPTER 4

THE CRAVING TRAP

"What you feed your mind determines your appetite. When it comes to food, this is literally true."

ZIG ZIGLAR

For a long time, I believed cravings were about willpower.

Most of us were taught that if we wanted sugar, caffeine, or processed food too badly, it meant we were weak, undisciplined, or "out of control."

But living with Hashimoto's Disease has shown me that cravings are not simply tests of willpower. While it took me a long time to change what I ate after Hashimoto's, it was hard because I loved pasta, pizza, and bread (after all, I am Italian), but I knew that if I was going to get better and healthier, things had to change. For a long time, I believed I just needed more discipline, that if I were stronger, I could resist these impulses. But the more I paid attention, the more I realized my body was not lacking willpower; it was lacking consistent support. Fluctuating energy, blood sugar imbalances, and underlying inflammation were driving those intense urges, making them feel almost impossible to ignore. Willpower can only carry you so far when your body is working against you. Once I shifted my focus to getting healthy and stronger, eating in a way that stabilized and supported my body, I noticed those cravings began to subside. It wasn't about trying harder, it was about finally giving my body what it needed so willpower didn't have to do all the work.

Hashimoto's also affected my mood in ways I didn't fully understand at first. There were days when I felt fatigued, overwhelmed, and easily irritated without a clear reason, and it was really frustrating not to be able to explain why. It often felt very unpredictable, like my emotions were shifting without warning. Over time, I began to pinpoint certain foods that affected my mood and energy, mostly related to sugar (carbohydrates). As I started supporting myself more consistently through nutrition and daily habits, I noticed my mood becoming much more stable.

If food can intensify symptoms for someone with Hashimoto's, imagine what is it doing to the rest of us quietly, daily, without a diagnosis to make it obvious?

CRAVINGS ARE SIGNALS, NOT FAILURES

Cravings are not moral weaknesses.

They are biological signals.

When the brain senses instability, low energy, stress, chemical imbalance, or overwhelm, it looks for the fastest relief possible.

That relief often comes in the form of:

- Sugar
- Refined carbs
- Ultra-processed foods
- Caffeine
- Comfort snacks

These foods work quickly.

They temporarily lift energy or mood.

But what comes next is the trap.

HOW THE CRAVING TRAP WORKS

Here's the cycle most people don't see:

1. The brain feels stressed, tired, or under-fueled
2. A craving appears (fast relief needed)
3. The food or drink provides a short boost
4. Blood sugar spikes
5. Stress hormones rise
6. The boost fades
7. Anxiety, fog, or irritability returns (and often stronger than before)
8. Another craving appears

This cycle doesn't just affect mood. It affects:

- Focus
- Patience
- Emotional regulation
- Sleep
- Self-trust

Watching my sister suffer with schizophrenia and diet, I saw how this cycle could magnify symptoms, not because she did something wrong, but because her system was already sensitive. It was a familiar scene, as I share a similar battle with Hashimoto's. Witnessing her struggle was a reminder that my own intense desire for inflammatory foods is a symptom of a sensitive system, making my health journey a constant battle against my own body.

Her body wasn't broken.

It was reactive.

And many of us are more reactive than we realize.

WHY SOME BRAINS ARE MORE SENSITIVE

Not all nervous systems respond the same way.

Some people can drink soda and feel fine. Others feel shaky, anxious, or overstimulated.

Some people can skip meals easily. Others feel emotionally unsteady if they do.

Mental health challenges, chronic stress, trauma, lack of sleep, and long-term poor nutrition can all make the brain less tolerant of spikes and crashes.

My sister's experience showed me this truth clearly:

> **The more vulnerable the mind, the more important the fuel.**

That applies to all of us, especially in hard seasons of life.

WHY WILLPOWER NEVER WINS THIS BATTLE

When the brain feels threatened, logic shuts down.

In survival mode, the brain does not care about:

- Long-term goals
- Health plans
- Discipline
- "What you should do"

It only wants relief.

People might say, "I don't know why I keep reaching for it."

But the real answer is simple: Their brains are trying to protect them.

Once I understood this, I stopped judging cravings, both mine and others.

I started listening instead.

THE SHIFT THAT CHANGES EVERYTHING: ADD BEFORE YOU RESTRICT

One of the most powerful lessons I learned is this:

> Restriction increases stress levels. Support calms the system.

Instead of saying:

- "Don't eat that."
- "Stop craving."
- "Cut this out."

Begin by asking:

- "What does the brain need right now?"
- "Is energy steady?"
- "Is the nervous system supported?"

This is where the Add-First Method comes in.

Before you remove anything, add:

- Protein
- Fiber

- Whole foods
- Hydration
- Regular meals

When the brain feels supported, cravings naturally soften. They may not disappear overnight, but they'll begin to lose their grip.

A COMPASSIONATE TRUTH

Watching my sister taught me this deeply:

> Food is not neutral for the mind. It can soothe, or it can amplify distress.

And when someone is already struggling, its effects are stronger, louder, and faster.

This isn't about blame. It's about awareness.

Once you see cravings as communication instead of failure, everything changes:

- You stop fighting your body
- You start working with it
- You make calmer choices
- You feel more in control

WHAT THIS MEANS FOR YOU

You don't need a diagnosis for food to affect your mind.

You only need to be human.

If you've ever felt:

- Anxious after eating
- Calm after a balanced meal
- Out of control around snacks
- Drained after sugar
- Relieved by protein
- Jittery from caffeine

Your body has been teaching you all along.

TOP BRAIN-BOOSTING IDEA

Avocados and Olive Oil: Powerful flavonoids and antioxidants boost blood flow and stabilize blood sugar.

Idea: cut a small avocado, put it in a bowl, and mash until creamy. Add some Redmond's salt along with some walnuts and blueberries. Perfect breakfast!

CHAPTER 5

THE CALM PLATE

"Nourishing yourself in a way that helps you blossom in the direction you want to go attainable, and you are worth the effort."

DEBORAH DAY

After watching how deeply food affected my sister's nervous system, one truth became impossible to ignore:

> **A calm mind begins with a calm body.**

When the body feels safe, nourished, and steady, the mind softens.

When the body feels stressed, depleted, or overwhelmed, the mind tightens.

Most people try to calm their thoughts first through positive thinking, breathing, or willpower. But for many of us, calm doesn't start in the mind.

It starts on the plate.

WHY CALM IS A PHYSICAL STATE

Calm isn't just an emotion. It's a biological state.

A calm body has:

- Stable blood sugar
- A supported nervous system
- Signals of safety instead of urgency

When those conditions are met, the mind naturally settles.

But when food creates spikes, drops, or stress signals, calm becomes almost impossible no matter how much you "try to relax."

I saw this clearly with my sister.

When her meals were steady and grounding, her body softened.

Her movements slowed.

Her nervousness eased.

Her anxiety felt quieter.

When meals were chaotic or highly processed, everything felt louder.

The difference wasn't discipline.

It was support.

THE CALM PLATE IS NOT A DIET

Let's be clear: The Calm Plate is not about perfection. It's not about cutting everything out. It's not about rules.

It's about sending safety signals to the brain.

Think of it as a template rather than a plan. A way to build meals that tell your nervous system:

"You're safe. You're supported. You can relax."

THE FOUR ELEMENTS OF THE CALM PLATE

A calm plate includes four simple elements

You don't have to get all four elements of a calm plate perfect every time. What matters most is staying consistent and making healthier choices the majority of the time.

1. Protein — The Anchor

Protein steadies blood sugar and helps the brain feel grounded.

Without it, energy rises fast and falls hard. I personally eat a lot of protein, not only because it benefits the mind, but because we need more protein as we get older to keep our skeletal muscles strong so they don't become fragile.

Protein can come in the form of:

- Eggs
- Fish
- Chicken
- Beans or lentils

- Greek yogurt
- Tofu
- Nuts or seeds

Protein doesn't make meals heavy.

It makes them stable.

2. Fiber & Color: The Soothers

Fiber feeds the gut, which communicates directly to the brain.

Colorful plants send calming, protective signals throughout the body.

Think:

- Vegetables
- Fruits
- Greens
- Beans
- Whole grains

Fiber slows digestion, smooths energy, and helps the mind feel less reactive.

3. Healthy Fats: The Nervous System Support

Your brain is made largely of fat.

To function smoothly, it needs to be fed the right kinds of fats.

Healthy fats help:

- Calm inflammation
- Support brain cell communication
- Increase feelings of satisfaction

Sources include:

- Olive oil
- Avocado
- Nuts
- Seeds
- Fatty fish

These fats help meals feel more satisfying, enhancing their flavor and ensuring you get the most nutrition out of your ingredients.

4. Carbohydrates: Chosen, Not Feared

Carbohydrates are not the enemy.

Unstable energy is.

When carbs are paired with protein, fiber, and fat, they offer calm instead of chaos.

Whole, slower-digesting carbs help the brain relax.

WHY THIS WORKS SO QUICKLY

Many people notice something surprising when they build calmer meals:

- Anxiety softens
- Cravings quiet down
- Focus improves
- Emotional reactions feel less intense
- Sleep becomes easier

This isn't because life suddenly changed.

It's because the nervous system stopped fighting for stability.

My sister's experience taught me something profound:

> When the body feels safe and supported, the mind doesn't have to shout.

THIS IS ESPECIALLY IMPORTANT IF YOU'RE SENSITIVE

If you:

- Feel anxious easily
- Are easily affected by caffeine or sugar
- Have mood swings
- Are often overwhelmed by stress
- Have a history of mental health struggles

Your brain may need more steadiness, not more discipline.

This kind of calm isn't created by restriction, but by consistency.

START SMALL, THAT'S WHERE CALM BEGINS

You don't need to change everything.

Start with:

- One calmer breakfast
- One steadier lunch
- One evening meal that supports relaxation

Small changes send big signals.

And when your nervous system starts to trust you again, calm follows naturally.

REFLECTION BOX: YOUR CALM PLATE AWARENESS

Take a moment to reflect on the following questions and write down your responses. Try to do so with curiosity instead of judgment.

1. After which meals do you feel most calm or grounded? What do those meals have in common?

2. Which foods make you feel anxious, jittery, or overwhelmed?

3. Do you notice a difference in your nervous system when you eat protein early in the day?

5. What is one simple change you could make this week to build a calmer plate?

Awareness is the first act of self-care.

TOP BRAIN-BOOSTING IDEA

Dark Chocolate-Flavonoids and antioxidants boost blood flow and memory. (When selecting your chocolate, choose 85%.)

Idea: Break dark chocolate into small pieces and sprinkle it over your favorite plain Greek yogurt.

CHAPTER 6

THE CLEAR MIND PLATE

"You yourself, as much as anybody in the entire universe, deserve your love and affection."

BUDDHA

Most people don't wake up hoping for perfection.

They wake up hoping for *clarity*.

They want to think straight. They want to focus without forcing it. They want their minds to feel sharp, not scattered.

And yet, many people live in a constant state of mental fog, telling themselves:

> *"This is just how my brain works."*

But what if it's not?

What if your brain is capable of far more clarity than you've been experiencing. What if the right kind of food is one of the missing pieces?

WHAT MENTAL CLARITY REALLY IS

A clear mind isn't about being "on" all the time.

It's about:

- Being able to focus without strain
- Thinking without overwhelm
- Making decisions without exhaustion
- Holding attention without distraction
- Feeling mentally present instead of spaced out

Clarity feels calm, not wired. Steady, not rushed.

And just like calm, clarity is not a personality trait.

It's a state, one your body helps create.

WHY THE BRAIN LOSES CLARITY

Mental fog often comes from one of three places:

- Unstable energy (spikes and crashes)
- Low-quality fuel (not enough building blocks)
- Over-stimulation (too much stress, caffeine, or sugar)

When the brain is constantly reacting, it can't focus. It's too busy trying to stay balanced.

I saw this clearly in my sister.

When her food was overstimulating—too sugary, too processed, or too caffeinated, her thoughts became faster but less organized. Her body looked alert, but her mind was scattered.

When her meals were steadier and more nourishing, her thinking slowed in a good way. She seemed more present. More grounded. More herself.

That's the difference between stimulation and clarity.

THE CLEAR MIND PLATE: FOCUS WITHOUT FORCE

The Clear Mind Plate is not about boosting energy.

It's about supporting the brain's ability to think clearly.

A clear mind comes from fuel that is steady and nutrient rich.

THE FOUR ELEMENTS OF THE CLEAR MIND PLATE

1. Protein: The Focus Foundation

Protein provides the building blocks your brain needs to make chemicals involved in attention, motivation, and alertness. Without enough protein, focus fades quickly, your motivation drops, and mental endurance suffers.

Protein helps the brain stay "online" longer without crashing.

2. Slow Carbohydrates: The Clarity Fuel

Your brain needs glucose, but it needs a slow and steady stream of it.

Whole, slower-digesting carbs help the brain think clearly over time.

Examples:

- Oats
- Sweet potatoes
- Beans
- Brown rice
- Quinoa
- Whole fruit

These carbs support thinking instead of hijacking it.

3. Healthy Fats: The Signal Sharpeners

Healthy fats help brain cells communicate smoothly.

When brain signals flow well, your thoughts feel organized, your focus feels natural, and your mental effort feels less strained.

These fats don't energize you instantly, they support you quietly and consistently.

4. Micro-nutrients: The Quiet Helpers

Your brain relies on vitamins and minerals to function well.

You don't need to know their names.

You just need *variety*.

Color on the plate usually means support in the brain.

WHY "MORE CAFFEINE" ISN'T THE ANSWER

When clarity fades, many people reach for caffeine.

Sometimes it helps.

Often it makes things worse.

Caffeine can:

- Increase alertness
- Increase anxiety
- Increase nervous system strain

If the brain is under-fueled, caffeine acts like a megaphone, loud, fast, and overwhelming.

A clear mind doesn't need to be pushed.

It needs to be supported.

WHAT A CLEAR MIND FEELS LIKE

People often describe it these ways:

- "I can think again."
- "I'm not fighting my brain.
- "Things feel simpler."

- "I don't feel so overwhelmed."

Clarity doesn't mean excitement.

It means *ease*.

While the Calm Plate and the Clear Mind Plate share many of the same foundation principles, they are designed with slightly different intentions in mind. Both focus on stabilizing the body through balanced nutrition, but each one supports a different mental state, one prioritizing emotional regulation and calm, and the other enhancing clarity, focus, and cognitive function. Understanding this distinction allows you to use each approach more intentionally, depending on what your mind and body need most in the moment.

WHEN TO USE THE CLEAR MIND PLATE

This plate is especially helpful:

- Before work or study
- During mentally demanding days
- When you feel scattered
- When focus feels fragile
- When caffeine isn't helping anymore

You don't need it at every meal.

Just when your mind needs support.

REFLECTION BOX: YOUR CLEAR MIND AWARENESS

Take a moment to reflect on the following questions and write down your responses. Try to do so with curiosity instead of judgment.

1. When during the day does your mind feel clearest? What have you usually eaten beforehand?

2. Which foods make you feel sharp at first but foggy later?

3. How does caffeine affect your focus versus your anxiety?

4. Do you notice clearer thinking when meals feel balanced instead of rushed?

5. What is one meal you could adjust this week to support mental clarity?

Clarity begins with awareness.

TOP BRAIN BOOSTING IDEA

Salmon (rich in omega-3s), sweet potato (slow-releasing carbs), arugula (for antioxidants), avocado (healthy fat), olive oil (reduces inflammation).

Idea: Grilled Salmon, half of a sweet potato, a handful of arugula, half of an avocado, roasted vegetables (broccoli or zucchini), olive oil, lemon juice, salt and pepper.

CHAPTER 7

THE STEADY MOOD PLATE

"Keep good company, read good books, love good things, and cultivate soul and body as faithfully as you can."

LOUISA MAY ALCOTT

Mood is one of the most misunderstood parts of being human.

People say things like:

- "I'm just moody."
- "That's my personality."
- "I've always been emotional."

But mood is not fixed.

It shifts regularly in response to what's happening inside the body.

And food plays a bigger role in that shift than most people realize.

WHAT A STEADY MOOD REALLY MEANS

A steady mood doesn't mean being happy all the time.

It means:

- Emotions feel manageable
- Reactions feel proportional
- Ups and downs feel softer
- You recover more quickly
- You feel more like *yourself*

A steady mood is not flat.

It's *supported.*

When the body feels stable, emotions don't have to swing so hard to get attention.

WHY MOOD FEELS UNPREDICTABLE

Mood swings often appear random, but they usually follow patterns.

Common triggers include:

- Blood sugar crashes
- Long gaps between meals
- Highly processed foods
- Too much sugar or caffeine

- Poor sleep
- Chronic stress

When the brain senses instability, it responds emotionally.

Not because you're weak but because it's trying to protect you.

I see this again and again with my sister.

When her meals are erratic or overstimulating, her emotions seem sharper and harder to manage.

When her food is steady and nourishing, her emotional world softens.

She isn't "better behaved."

She is better supported.

THE STEADY MOOD PLATE: EMOTIONAL SUPPORT THROUGH FOOD

A Steady Mood Plate is designed to smooth emotional highs and lows by reducing the internal chaos caused by blood sugar spikes, nutrient gaps, and inflammation. Mineral-rich foods, especially those high in magnesium like dark chocolate and leafy greens, play a big role in supporting your nervous system and promoting a more relaxed, stable mood. Olive oil also helps with calming the brain. Eating all those highly processed foods, like packaged snacks, sweets, sodas, and foods with added sugar like corn syrup, can lead to a quick burst of energy followed by a sharp drop. When these foods are consumed on a regular basis, they can make emotions feel more unpredictable and harder to manage, amplifying the very highs and lows you're trying to avoid. These foods hurt you in more ways than you think, negatively affecting not just your mind but your overall health. Made with chemicals, they are poison to your body. If you ever get a chance, look at the ingredients in these foods, and you will know what I am talking about. They are not even real food.

THE FOUR ELEMENTS OF THE STEADY MOOD PLATE

1. Regular Meals , The Emotional Stabilizer

Skipping meals or eating unpredictably stresses the brain.

A stressed brain reacts emotionally.

Regular meals:

- Reduce mood dips
- Support patience
- Improve emotional resilience

Your brain likes rhythm.

Consistency builds trust.

2. Protein, The Mood Buffer

Protein helps provide the building blocks for brain chemicals involved in mood regulation.

Without enough protein:

- Emotions feel louder
- Stress feels heavier
- Motivation dips

Protein doesn't numb emotions, it helps balance them.

3. Whole Carbohydrates: The Emotional Grounding

Carbs help support calming brain pathways when chosen wisely.

Whole, slower-digesting carbs like sweet potatoes or beans:

- Reduce irritability
- Support emotional steadiness
- Help prevent mood crashes

The goal isn't elimination.

It's balance.

4. Minerals & Fats: The Nervous System Support

Your nervous system needs minerals and healthy fats to regulate stress.

When these are lacking:

- Anxiety increases
- Tension rises

- Emotional regulation feels harder

Nourishment creates emotional safety.

WHY EMOTIONAL EATING IS NOT A FAILURE

People often eat emotionally because they're trying to self-soothe. Food can help accomplish this, but only temporarily.

The problem isn't emotional eating. It's relying on something that doesn't truly support or stabilize what's happening underneath. When the body isn't nourished in a consistent, balanced way, emotions can feel more intense, and food becomes a quick form of relief rather real support. The goal isn't to eliminate emotional eating, but to create a foundation where your body and mind feel steady enough that you don't have to depend on it as your primary way of coping.

When the body is nourished:

- Emotions soften naturally
- Urges lose intensity
- Self-trust increases

You don't need to fight your emotions.

You need to support the system experiencing them.

WHAT A STEADY MOOD FEELS LIKE

People describe it as:

- "I'm less reactive."
- "Things don't bother me as much."
- "I bounce back faster."
- "I feel more grounded."
- "I don't feel so fragile."

This is what emotional nourishment feels like.

WHEN TO USE THE STEADY MOOD PLATE

This plate is especially helpful:

- During stressful seasons
- Around hormonal shifts
- When emotions feel intense
- When mood swings feel frequent
- When life feels heavy

It's not about control.

It's about self-respect.

REFLECTION BOX: YOUR MOOD AWARENESS

1. When do your mood dips or spikes tend to happen during the day?

2. How long after eating do emotional shifts appear?
3. Do skipped meals or sugary foods affect your mood?
4. Which meals make you feel emotionally steady afterward?
5. What is one way you could support your mood with food this week?

Write your answers down.

Understanding your mood is an act of self-respect.

TOP BRAIN-BOOSTING IDEAS

Chicken and Avocado offer healthy fats and steady protein for neurotransmitters. They also reduce inflammation.

Idea: Take an avocado, smash it until creamy, then add onions, olive oil, salt, and pepper. Meanwhile, cook chicken breast. When the chicken is fully cooked and cooled, shred it into small pieces. Then add the olive oil and avocado mix to the chicken. A healthy lunch or dinner without using store-bought mayonnaise.

CHAPTER 8

SLEEP IS A FOOD ISSUE (AND FOOD IS A SLEEP ISSUE)

"If you have the ability to love, love yourself first."

CHARLES BUKOWSKI

Most people think sleep problems begin at bedtime.

They focus on:

- Pillows
- Mattresses
- Screens
- Supplements
- Nighttime routines

But for many people, sleep trouble starts much earlier in the day, sometimes as early as breakfast.

Sleep is not just about what you do at night. It's about how supported your body feels all day.

Once you understand this, sleep stops feeling mysterious and starts feeling manageable.

WHY THE BRAIN CAN'T SLEEP WHEN THE BODY IS STRESSED

Your brain only sleeps well when it feels safe.

Not emotionally safe, but biologically safe.

Your brain stays alert if your body senses:

- Low fuel
- Blood sugar crashes
- Excess stimulation
- Inflammation
- Stress hormones still circulating

It doesn't know it's bedtime.

It only knows something feels off.

That's when people experience:

- Trouble falling asleep
- Waking in the middle of the night
- Racing thoughts

- Early-morning anxiety
- Restless sleep
- Feeling tired but wired

These aren't failures of discipline.

They're signals.

WHAT I NOTICED WITH MY SISTER

With my sister, sleep was one of the first things to unravel when her eating habits were chaotic.

Sugar drinks late in the day. Highly processed snacks. Long gaps between meals. Too much caffeine.

Her nights became restless. Her body stayed tense. Her anxiety carried into the night.

When her meals were steadier and more nourishing, something shifted.

She didn't sleep perfectly, but she slept more peacefully. Her body softened at night instead of staying on high alert.

That showed me something important:

> Sleep doesn't improve when we try to force it. It improves when the nervous system feels supported.

THE DAYTIME CHOICES THAT SHAPE YOUR NIGHT

Sleep quality is influenced by events that occur hours before bedtime.

MORNING & MIDDAY FUEL

If you under-fuel early in the day:

- Stress hormones rise
- Blood sugar becomes unstable
- The nervous system stays reactive

That stress doesn't disappear at night.

It lingers.

AFTERNOON CRASHES

Late-day sugar or caffeine can:

- Spike energy artificially
- Delay natural tiredness
- Increase nighttime restlessness

EVENING MEALS

A chaotic or overly light dinner can:

- Trigger nighttime hunger
- Cause blood sugar dips
- Wake you during the night

Sleep needs steady support, not extremes.

THE SLEEP-SUPPORTING PLATE

The goal of a sleep-supporting plate is not to weigh you down. It's to make you feel more grounded.

A good evening meal:

- Feels satisfying
- Feels calming
- Doesn't overstimulate
- Helps the body relax

It often includes:

- Protein (for stability)
- Whole carbohydrates (for calm)
- Healthy fats (for satiety)
- Simple, familiar foods

Your body should feel nourished, not rushed.

WHY NIGHTTIME CRAVINGS OFTEN APPEAR

Late-night cravings are rarely about hunger alone.

They often show up when:

- The body is under-fueled
- Stress hormones are high

- Blood sugar drops
- The nervous system seeks comfort

Food becomes a tool for calming.

Instead of fighting cravings, ask:

> "What support did my body miss today?"

That question changes everything.

SLEEP IS A SIGNAL OF BALANCE

Good sleep is often a sign that:

- Your energy was steady
- Your meals were supportive
- Your nervous system felt safe
- Your brain trusted the environment

When sleep improves, people often notice:

- Better mood
- Fewer cravings
- Clearer thinking
- More resilience to stress

Sleep doesn't just restore the body.

It resets the mind.

LET SLEEP BE A RESULT, NOT A GOAL

Trying harder to sleep often backfires.

Supporting your body throughout the day helps you sleep naturally.

You don't need perfection. You need consistency.

Small shifts, including earlier nourishment, steadier meals, and calmer evenings, add up quickly.

REFLECTION BOX: YOUR SLEEP AWARENESS

1. How do you usually feel before bed, calm, wired, hungry, restless?
2. Do your sleep struggles follow days of skipped meals or high stress?
3. How does caffeine timing affect your nights?
4. What evening meals help you feel grounded and ready for rest?
5. What is one daytime change that might support better sleep this week?

Write your answers down.

Sleep listens to how you treat yourself all day.

TOP BRAIN-BOOSTING IDEA

Ground Turkey: In a pan, mix ground turkey with your choice of beans. Add some chopped onions and spinach and add a half a sweet potato.

Chamomile tea: naturally calming

Idea: Boil water with chamomile tea and a little honey to enhance flavor. Perfect for relaxation.

CHAPTER 9

YOUR GUT TALKS TO YOUR BRAIN

"It's not selfish to love yourself, take care of yourself, and to make your happiness a priority. It's necessary."

MANDY HALE

Most people think thoughts start in the brain.

But many of the signals that shape your mood, clarity, and emotional state begin much lower, in the gut.

Your gut is not just a digestion system. It's a communication center. And it's talking to your brain all day long.

Most people just don't know how to listen.

THE GUT-BRAIN CONVERSATION

Your gut and brain are in constant contact through:

- Nerves
- Hormones

- Immune signals
- Chemical messengers

This connection is so strong that the gut is often called "the second brain."

When the gut is calm, the brain often feels calmer too.

When the gut is inflamed or stressed, the brain feels it.

This helps explain why digestive discomfort and mental discomfort so often travel together.

HOW GUT STRESS SHOWS UP IN THE MIND

Gut imbalance doesn't always look like stomach pain.

It can show up as:

- Anxiety
- Brain fog
- Irritability
- Low mood
- Fatigue
- Feeling "off" without knowing why

The brain interprets gut distress as a threat.

And when the brain senses threat, it shifts into protection mode emotionally and mentally.

WHAT I SAW WITH MY SISTER

When my sister's digestion was unsettled, her mental state often followed.

Certain foods caused visible changes:

- Increased nervousness
- Heightened anxiety
- Restlessness
- Emotional volatility

Other foods seemed to ground her:

- Simple meals
- Familiar foods
- Balanced plates
- Regular eating times

Her mind wasn't calm because someone told her to calm down.

It calmed because her body felt safer.

That connection became impossible to ignore.

WHY THE GUT HOLDS SO MUCH POWER

Your gut:

- Produces a large portion of mood-related chemicals

- Houses trillions of microbes that influence brain signals
- Acts as a gatekeeper between food and bloodstream

When the gut feels overwhelmed, the brain receives stress signals.

When the gut feels supported, the brain often responds with clarity and ease.

This is not a coincidence. It's biology.

COMMON GUT STRESSORS MOST PEOPLE MISS

Many people unknowingly stress their gut every day.

Common triggers include:

- Highly processed foods
- Eating too quickly
- Eating while stressed
- Skipping meals
- Constant snacking without nourishment
- Artificial additives

Over time, the gut loses its sense of safety.

And the brain mirrors that instability.

THE CALM GUT APPROACH

A calm gut doesn't require extreme diets.

It thrives on:

- Simplicity
- Consistency
- Familiar foods
- Regular meals
- Gentle preparation

Sometimes less variety brings more peace.

Healing doesn't always mean adding more, sometimes it means giving your body what it's been missing all along.

Sometimes it means reducing stress.

HOW TO SUPPORT THE GUT-MIND CONNECTION

Start small.

- Eat without rushing
- Chew more slowly
- Choose meals that feel grounding
- Notice how foods make you feel, not how they're labeled
- Respect your body's signals

Your gut responds to kindness.

So does your mind.

WHAT A CALM GUT FEELS LIKE MENTALLY

People often describe:

- Less anxiety after meals
- Clearer thinking
- Improved mood
- A sense of internal stability
- Fewer emotional swings

Mental calm often begins in the belly.

REFLECTION BOX: YOUR GUT AWARENESS

1. How do you usually feel mentally after eating: calm, rushed, foggy, energized?
2. Are there foods that consistently make you feel unsettled?
3. Do you eat under stress or distraction most days?
4. Which meals leave you feeling grounded and clear?
5. What is one small change that could support your gut this week?

Write your answers down.

Your gut has been speaking to you for a long time.

TOP BRAIN-BOOSTING IDEA

Kefir is gut-friendly and is a natural source of probiotics.

Idea: Mix kefir, frozen berries, a banana, and honey in a blender until smooth and enjoy!

CHAPTER 10

FOOD, TRAUMA, AND THE NERVOUS SYSTEM

"Talk to yourself like you would to someone you love."

BRENE BROWN

Trauma doesn't only live in memory.

It lives in the body.

In tension.

In digestion.

In sleep patterns.

In reactions that feel bigger than the moment.

And very often, it lives in a nervous system.

Food interacts with that system every single day.

WHAT TRAUMA REALLY DOES TO THE BODY

Trauma teaches the body one main lesson:

> "Stay alert."

Even long after the danger has passed, the body may remain on guard.

This can look like:

- Anxiety without a clear reason
- Sudden emotional reactions
- Digestive discomfort
- Trouble sleeping
- Feeling constantly tense or overwhelmed

This is not a weakness.

It is a mode of self-protection that you never realized was safe to release.

WHY THE NERVOUS SYSTEM CARES ABOUT FOOD

Your nervous system's job is to keep you alive.

It constantly asks:

- Am I safe?
- Do I have enough?
- Is something wrong?

Food answers those questions quietly but powerfully.

The nervous system stays on high alert when nourishment is:

- Inconsistent
- Highly stimulating
- Chaotic
- Stress-driven

The nervous system can begin to soften when nourishment is:

- Steady
- Predictable
- Grounding
- Supportive

WHAT I OBSERVED WITH MY SISTER

My sister's nervous system was always working overtime.

Certain foods and drinks didn't just affect her digestion, they affected her entire state.

After certain meals:

- Her body became restless
- Her anxiety increased
- Her thoughts raced
- Her emotional world felt fragile

But when her meals were simple, balanced, and regular, something changed.

She didn't become "calm" overnight.

But she became less activated, which meant:

- More emotional space
- Fewer spirals
- A body that could rest

Food didn't heal her trauma, but it stopped adding fuel to it.

TRAUMA AND CONTROL AROUND FOOD

Many people with trauma develop complicated relationships with food.

Some intentionally eat foods that will make them lose control.

Some overeat to feel safe.

Some numb emotions with certain foods.

These are not bad habits.

They are coping strategies.

Food becomes a tool when the nervous system doesn't trust the environment.

Understanding this removes shame.

HOW TO USE FOOD AS NERVOUS SYSTEM SUPPORT

The goal is not perfection.

The goal is safety.

Supportive nourishment looks like:

- Eating regularly
- Avoiding extreme highs and lows
- Choosing foods that feel familiar
- Eating in calm environments when possible
- Listening to body signals

Predictability tells the nervous system:

> "You're okay right now."

THE POWER OF GENTLE REPETITION

Trauma healing is not about dramatic change.

It's about repetition.

Each steady meal says:

- You will be fed
- You don't have to panic
- There is enough

Over time, the nervous system learns.

WHAT REGULATION FEELS LIKE

When the nervous system feels supported, people often notice:

- Fewer intense reactions
- More emotional space
- Improved digestion
- Better sleep
- A sense of internal safety

This is regulation.

Not numbness.

Not control.

Just support.

FOOD IS NOT THE CURE, BUT IT IS THE ENVIRONMENT

Food doesn't erase trauma.

But it does create an environment where healing becomes possible.

A stressed body cannot heal.

A supported body can begin the process.

REFLECTION BOX: NERVOUS SYSTEM AWARENESS

1. Do certain foods make you feel more anxious or overstimulated?
2. Do skipped meals increase emotional reactivity for you?
3. How does your body feel after calm, balanced meals?
4. Are your food patterns driven by safety or stress?
5. What is one way you could make meals feel safer this week?

Write your answers down.

Your nervous system is listening.

TOP BRAIN-BOOSTING IDEA

Chicken Soup: A great comfort meal

Idea: Add olive oil, diced celery, and carrots to a pot over medium heat. Add garlic to the pot and cook until golden. Add your favorite chicken stock and season with some rosemary, salt, and pepper. Bring to a boil. You can add an already cooked chicken rotisserie—just shred the chicken into the pot and let it cook. Enjoy.

CONCLUSION

As you close this book, I hope you walk away with this simple awareness:

> What you eat can shape how you feel physically, mentally, and emotionally.

Food is not just something we consume.

It is something we experience.

The right choices can help you feel clearer, calmer, more energized, and more connected to yourself. They can lift brain fog, steady your emotions, and give you a sense of strength from the inside out.

When your body feels supported, your mind often returns to balance with it. You rediscover a sense of equilibrium and clarity.

You don't need perfection to feel amazing. You only need awareness. Paying attention to how different foods make you feel gives you the power to choose what truly serves you.

When you nourish your body with intention, you may find yourself feeling lighter, sharper, and more grounded. Sometimes you'll even feel on top of the world.

Let awareness become your guide.

Let food become your ally.

And let feeling good become something you allow yourself to experience every single day.

ABOUT THE AUTHOR

Sena Lirasso is a wellness-focused non-fiction author with a deep passion for understanding how the mind works and how everyday choices shape mental clarity, emotional balance, and overall well-being.

While working demanding 11-hour days as a spotter driver, Sena continues to dedicate her time and energy to learning, writing, and researching the powerful connection between food, exercise, and mental health. Her passion for understanding the mind outweighs even the busiest schedules, driving her commitment to share knowledge that can genuinely improve people's lives.

Her writing explores how a healthy diet, intentional movement, and small daily habits influence how we think, feel, and function. What began as personal curiosity has become a meaningful mission: helping others support both their mental and physical health with compassion and awareness.

Sena's latest work, *Mind-Food Secret*, is her second book and builds on these ideas by uncovering the often-overlooked relationship between nourishment and the mind.

When she isn't working or writing, Sena enjoys studying neuroscience, wellness practices, and the simple routines that help people feel clearer, calmer, and more connected to themselves.

www.ingramcontent.com/pod-product-compliance
Ingram Content Group UK Ltd.
Pitfield, Milton Keynes, MK11 3LW, UK
UKHW040232290926
15471UKWH00002B/140

9 798996 140220